"During his ministry on earth, Jesus spent a significant amount of energy inviting those who followed him to be radical risk takers. Not to take the kinds of risks that are prodded by foolishness but rather the kinds of risks that are rooted in faith and driven by love. Both Julie and G are those kinds of risk takers in very different and very unique ways. The story being told here, both in the narrative and the recipes, is the kind that invites us into a deeper understanding of the heart of a God. It is an opportunity to explore the layers and complexities which exist in a love-rooted, faith-driven kind of risk taking. It is a book I will revisit over and over again."

—Heather Avis, author, podcaster, and narrative shifter

"Recipes for Risk" is a beautifully vulnerable peek into how one family found purpose and passion in foster care. Your heart will resonate deeply with each chapter of their unfolding story as their world collides with the worlds of kids who need loving and safe homes. You'll walk away with some amazing recipes to enjoy and some deeply profound things to consider about your own life and how it might be used to love some of the most pushed aside and forgotten among you.

—Jason Johnson, author of *ReFraming Foster Care*

If you're like so many of us who have either thought or said out loud that there has to be more to life than this, then Recipes for Risk is the book for you. It's hard to believe a book so small could throw such a relatable punch. Caring for the vulnerable kids among us through adoption, fostering, or respite-care may be one of the most uncharted terrains we could walk, because there really is no map, but Julie Mavis walks ahead of us in an honest and brave way. Recipes for Risk is such a human account for the sacred and scary things we're called to do to bring healing to the world - and even healing to ourselves.

—Amber Haines, author of *Wild in the Hollow*

"Julie Mavis is one of the most inspiring people I know! Her compassion, her faith, and her compelling sense of purpose are beautifully shared in Recipes for Risk. True to her nature, this memoir is less about her and more about the countless lives influenced by her extraordinary heart. You'll be inspired and challenged… and hopefully encouraged to believe that small steps of courage can have remarkable impact."

—Jenni Catron, author, speaker, and founder of *The 4Sight Group*

Recipes for Risk

Finding Purpose and Passion in Foster Care

by Julie Mavis

Photographs and cover image by Annie Marek-Barta, a young woman who aged out of foster care. (Instagram: @anniemarekbarta)

Copyright © 2020 Julie Mavis All Rights Reserved

ISBN: 9798580032948

ALL PROFITS OF THIS BOOK GO TO AMERICA'S KIDS BELONG AND OUR DREAM MAKERS PROGRAM.

TABLE OF CONTENTS

PREFACE..11

Chapter 1: The Missing Ingredient 13

    Mango and Avocado Salsa 16

Chapter 2: I'm No Mother Teresa 19

    Carnitas With Purple Cabbage Slaw................... 22

Chapter 3: Finding My Calcutta 25

    Homemade Pesto 28

Chapter 4: Baby Steps That Led To A Baby.......31

    Oat Milk Matcha Latte 33

Chapter 5: First Love 35

    Sweet and Salty Granola 38

Chapter 6: Hard To Place 41

    Confit Chicken with Potatoes and Demi Sauce
    43

Chapter 7: A Face And A Voice..........................47

    Acai Bowls 51

Chapter 8: Be Mine 53

Beets Beets Salad 56

Chapter 9: Breaking Bread 59
Sunnyside-Up Toast 64

Chapter 10: Scraps Of Life 67
Ribollita - Tuscan Vegetable Soup and
Homemade Croutons 71

Chapter 11: Our Own Hell's Kitchen 73
Fresh Herb Roasted Tomatoes 77

Chapter 12: G: On My Own 79
Manchego Infused Oil Tapas 80

Chapter 13: "Traumatism" 83
Sweet & Spicy Barba"cola" Tacos Topped with
Marinated Vegetables 87

Chapter 14: Selfless Love 91
Simple and Raw Protein Balls 94

Chapter 15: Be Brave 97
Seoul Sliders 101

*"Tell me,
what is it you plan to do
with your one
wild and precious life?"*

Mary Oliver

PREFACE

This is a well-seasoned stew of stories of our family's journey through foster care full of love and heartbreak. My heart is to shine a light on kids who have been in foster care in a creative way and to point you towards Jesus. So this book is part my memoir and part cookbook from a young man who aged out of foster care and who has lived with us for the past three-plus years. He doesn't use measurements or timers, so I did the best I could to share with you some of his most scrumptious creations as well as a few recipes we created together (which is one of the best things we do to connect with each other). Cooking together connected us, brought healing, and built trust between us.

My prayer is that you will try a recipe or two. Open a bottle of wine. Connect with your family, laugh, be grateful and consider making room for one more at your table.

Bon appétit!

CHAPTER 1
THE MISSING INGREDIENT

"God-ordained passions often break our hearts. And they can seem like an overwhelming burden to bear. But pursuing our passions is the key to living a fruitful and fulfilling life. It is the thing that wakes us up early in the morning and keeps us up late at night. It is the thing that turns a career into a calling. It is the thing that gives us goosebumps--Wild Goose bumps. And nothing will bring you greater joy."
Mark Batterson

On the outside, my life was perfect. Living with my husband and two daughters in Southern California, I was a part-time entrepreneur with a small jewelry business who spent a majority of my excess time playing beach volleyball. It was a true California dream. My husband, Brian, and I had created a predictable and comfortable life for ourselves and our girls, Elle and Shelby. They were adorable and (lucky for us) best friends. Every day, the girls and I would walk down the hill from our two-story house to their elementary school, and I would wave at them until they disappeared into the crowd of their friends. But each day, when I got back home, I experienced a restlessness that didn't seem to relent.

I was grateful for what we had, but I also felt like there had to be more to the life I was living -- not more stuff, but more meaning. My friends and neighbors were quintessential middle-class families -- minivans and all. We all volunteered at the school, shopped at Target, made cookies for our kids, watched each other's pets when we were out of town, and babysat each other's kids. We were all "nice" moms. I found myself surrounded by people that looked like me, acted like me, and were also comfortable like me. My life really didn't look much different from our non-Christian neighbors. I was a Christian, yet the only thing that seemed to set me apart was a few hours on Sunday.

At this same time, I was replaying the words my doctor spoke when he said, "I'm sorry, there's no heartbeat," when we found out we had miscarried a child. I also was still grieving the loss of my parents' recent divorce. I struggled with shame, low self-esteem, and inadequacy and tried numbing the pain with busyness, material things, hobbies, and poor choices that led me down some dark roads. I felt lost and like something was missing, like I was disqualified from making a difference in life.

Feeling desperate for change, I knew I needed to create space in my life to be intentional about hearing from God again. One morning, after spending some time in prayer, I got distracted (as usual) and noticed one of Brian's books laying on the coffee table called, The Purpose Driven Life by Pastor Rick Warren. The word "purpose" grabbed my attention, so I picked it up and started to read. I gravitated towards sections recounting Kay Warren's passion for orphans after she realized there were so many orphans in the world without a place to call home. A hazy memory hit me with stunning clarity. At one point in my past, caring for orphans was my purpose too, and I had lost that passion and purpose.

Reawakened to the call, I wondered what this would look like in my life now. What about my family? What about the safety of our sacred bubble? I tried to remember the last time I saw an orphanage that wasn't in a movie. Where were these children I felt drawn to protect? There were no sad children begging for change on the side of the road in my town. The invisibility of the need had blinded me, but it wouldn't for long.

Mango and Avocado Salsa

Mangos + avocado + jalapeno + red onion + red bell pepper + fresh cilantro + rice vinegar + lime + salt & pepper

Slice up 3 fresh mangos and one avocado. Chop up a jalapeño (amount depends on how spicy you want it), some red onion, red bell pepper, and fresh cilantro. Add in a couple of splashes of rice vinegar. Squeeze in some lime. Add salt and pepper to taste. Toss together. It's delicious on fish or on chicken made with G's chicken spice mix.

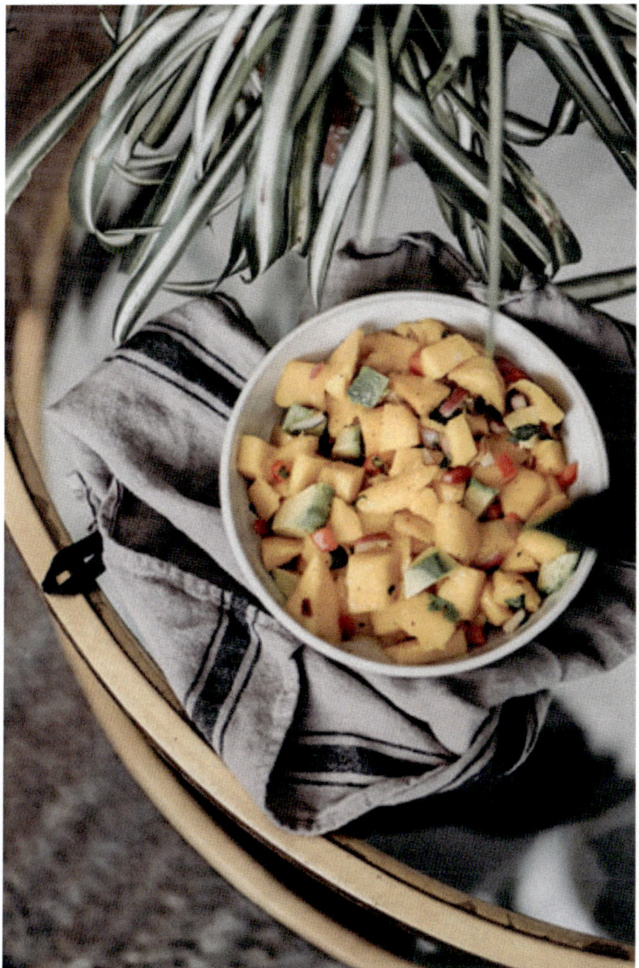

CHAPTER 2
I'M NO MOTHER TERESA

"The place God calls you to is the place where your deep gladness and the world's deep hunger meet."

Frederick Buechner

....

I said yes to the Baja Mexico mission trip for the following reasons: yummy tacos, the opportunity to buy an authentic poncho, and because it meant a bus ride long enough to make out with a boy. Plus, my dad was a pastor so I was expected to go. These were the wholesome reasons I worked at an orphanage the summer after my sixteenth birthday. I was selfish and boy crazy. I believed mascara was the greatest invention ever (still do). This trip, like all of life in high school, was about me.

I remember standing in the sweltering sun in the middle of the open courtyard lined by buildings along the outer edge where the kids would eat and sleep in slivers of shade. I listened to the delighted giggles of the kids playing with my church friends—some laughing, some crying because they were tagged in a game of kickball. Most of them were running around with ragged clothes, barefoot, with dirt caked all over their bodies. There wasn't much food and their wiry arms and legs looked frail as they played games in the dust. While looking into their big, brown eyes and knowing they were abandoned, my heart felt something it had never felt before: brokenness.

Even in my utter self-absorption, God was showing me the things he sees and making me feel what he feels. From somewhere deep inside of me, I heard God's voice say, "Care for orphans."

My heart heard it loud and clear. I had no idea what to make of the fact that I heard God say something directed right at me, but I felt it through my entire being that the voice I heard was God's calling (or his plan) for my life.

I didn't have a theology or framework for what happened at that moment. No one in my family or my church talked about hearing from God, nor did we talk about spending time with Him in spiritual practices like solitude. We talked about a lot of good things, just not these things. I couldn't articulate it until much later, but I did know at least on some level that this event was life-changing.

I said yes to the Baja Mexico mission trip for myself, but I left with an entirely new view of the "other" in the world. The lost, forgotten, abandoned, and neglected now had names and faces and dirt underneath their fingernails. I felt the brokenness, but I also felt more alive than ever before.

A few years later, as a single adult, I worked all summer at another orphanage in the interior of Mexico with a couple hundred kids. It was hard, sweaty, and dirty work, and I loved it. I knew I was doing the work God wanted me to do.

A few years later, I got married to Brian, and we moved to Tegucigalpa, Honduras. While Brian taught English at the University of Honduras during the day, I spent my time at an orphanage for terminally ill children called "Amor Y Vida" (Love and Life). Most of the children there were emaciated and balding from chemotherapy. They subsisted on rabbit soup, took ice-cold showers with no towels, and slept on cots with only a thin blanket for warmth. One of my responsibilities at the orphanage was washing the lice from their hair when they arrived and ended up with lice as well. I had to do this outside with a hose and cold water. It seemed like every few months one of the kids would pass away, and we would all drive out to a field to bury them. No family ever attended, just the other kids who were living there. I was exhausted and weary with grief. Most days after I left the orphanage, I would get into the taxi and sob the whole way back to our apartment.

After carrying so much pain that year, when we

moved back to the States, we settled in for a more comfortable life.

Carnitas With Purple Cabbage Slaw

Pork + Cinnamon Sticks + Bay leaves + Cloves + Nutmeg + Onion + Garlic + Brown sugar + Salt and Pepper + Modella Beer + Fresh Oranges + Organic Milk

Dry ingredients:

2 large handfuls of organic light brown sugar

Whole black peppercorns - crushed

2 whole cinnamon sticks

1-2 dry bay leaves

2-3 whole cloves

1 dash nutmeg

1 small white onion, cut into thirds

Add Kosher salt

1 whole bulb of garlic

Mix together the above dry ingredients. Add in your pork shoulder and cure it for 4-6 hrs in the refrigerator.

Take out of the refrigerator and discard any

liquids.

Then in a separate bowl add in your wet ingredients below.

1 bottle of Modella beer 12 oz Negra dark

3-4 fresh oranges (squeeze in the juice and throw in the rinds as well)

Around 2 cups whole organic milk

Wisk it all together and pour over the pork shoulder and the remains from the dry ingredients

Marinade 6 hrs or overnight

Cooking pork:

Bring a large pan to high heat and add canola oil so it doesn't stick. Sear the pork on all sides so it is a golden brown. Add in the onions, oranges, and spices and keep wet marinade separate. Add enough canola oil to cover the meat and add in the leftover marinade and bring it to a boil. Put foil on top and throw it in the oven at 285 for roughly 4-6 hrs until tender.

Purple cabbage and carrot slaw: Cabbage + Carrots + Cilantro + Lime + Oil + Salt and Pepper

Shred carrots and purple cabbage. Chop your cilantro. Combine in a bowl. 2 to 1 ratio on the lime and oil. Add salt and pepper to taste. Mix well.

Top your carnitas with purple cabbage slaw + fresh limes + cotija cheese

CHAPTER 3
FINDING MY CALCUTTA

"Stay where you are. Find your own Calcutta. Find the sick, the suffering, and the lonely right there where you are—in your own homes and in your own families, in your workplaces, and in your schools. You can find Calcutta all over the world if you have the eyes to see. Everywhere, wherever you go, you find people who are unwanted, unloved, uncared for, just rejected by society-completely forgotten, completely left alone."

Mother Teresa

I quickly got on my computer and typed in "Orphanages in California." Nothing popped up. How could there be orphanages less than an hour away in Baja Mexico, and yet none in our area? My online queries led me back to the same conclusion: the need was somewhere else.

A few hours later, I picked up the local paper to take a quick skim of the latest news when I noticed an ad for a thrift store raising money for foster care. The thrift store happened to be close to where I lived, and I had never heard of foster care before. I decided to check it out.

A few local women were running the store. As I skimmed the rows of used onesies, plastic fire trucks, tattered books, highchairs, and newly donated items like diapers and bottles, the women gave me a little tour and told me their mission was to raise money for foster care. They explained that children whose parents were unable to care for them were temporarily placed in foster homes until the county could figure out what to do next to best protect them. Reasons for removal include parents being incarcerated, domestic violence or drug use in the home, and the occurrence of physical or sexual abuse. While sharing this information, one of the women was feeding a premature foster baby while her other foster kids were playing with some toys in the corner. Momentarily distracted by a customer at the register, she asked me to continue feeding the baby while she rang them up. I took the baby instinctively. It had been so long since my own girls were this little - although they were never this little - and I was taken aback by how light and fragile this bundle was. I felt a lump in my throat. My heart was pounding a little faster, and my head swirled. I was so sad for this vulnerable baby, made small by someone else's addiction. I was scared I wasn't holding him right - wasn't caring for him correctly in my tiny moment of responsibility. Mostly, I wanted to be like these ladies: strong, committed, and compassionate. They were all in.

That stirring of renewed desire pulsed louder in their presence, and it made me uncomfortable. Although I enjoyed being with these moms, I left quickly to hit the beach again for some more volleyball. After a few good games and feeling the sand between my toes, I grabbed my flip flops, towel, and headed to get the girls from school. Even with a to-do list gnawing at the back of my head (Elle's dance class, Shelby's homework, chili and cornbread for dinner), I couldn't stop thinking about those foster kids at the thrift store. It was then that I had a vivid flashback of when I was working at the orphanage in Mexico as a single woman. I stayed in a beat-up trailer next to the orphanage's kitchen where the smell of fresh-made tortillas drifted through my window, but I wasn't just remembering the tortillas. I was remembering the trauma I had buried deep inside me, and now it flooded to the surface.

One afternoon, I found the courage to speak with the director of the orphanage, an older man with thinly-rimmed glasses. Seizing a rare opportunity when he emerged from his office, I asked my burning question: "How did all of their parents die?"

"They didn't all die," he said, a little shocked at my naivety. "Most of them have parents," he went on to explain, "but they are in jail, or they are prostitutes, or they are addicts. Possibly they abused their kids, or they severely neglected or abandoned the kids."

This flashback became a revelation: in other countries, vulnerable kids were placed in orphanages, but in the U.S. these kids were placed in foster care -- either with foster families or in group facilities. The kids I had longed to care for were not far away in other countries. These were the SAME kids right here in our midst! I felt like I had cracked a major code.

The gravitational pull of that stirring from long ago wasn't drawing me away to a third world country -- it was drawing me towards the vulnerable in my own city, and the need was all around me.

Homemade Pesto

Fresh Basil + Garlic + Olive Oil + Pine Nuts +

Parmesan cheese + salt + pepper

In your food processor, add in around two cups of fresh basil (it's easy to grow or you can just buy it fresh), 2 -3 garlic cloves, ½ cup olive oil, a small handful of pine nuts, ½ - ¾ cup parmesan cheese, and kosher salt and pepper to taste. Blend together. You can add in lemon zest and substitute walnuts or sunflower seeds for the pine nuts, or throw in a touch of spinach with your basil. Great on pasta, chicken or on toasted yummy bread with tomatoes and avocados.

CHAPTER 4
BABY STEPS THAT LED TO A BABY

"For I was hungry and you gave me food, I was thirsty and you gave me drink, I was a stranger and you welcomed me, I was naked and you clothed me, I was sick and you visited me, I was in prison and you came to me.' Then the righteous will answer him, saying, 'Lord, when did we see you hungry and feed you, or thirsty and give you drink? And when did we see you as a stranger and welcome you, or naked and clothe you? And when did we see you sick or in prison and visit you?'"

Jesus in Matthew 25:35-40

....

It started with a baby step. Unwilling to fully part with the routine of my work and personal life, I decided to volunteer at the thrift store part-time. I sorted and hung children's clothes, stacked stuffed animals, and helped ring up customers on a register that had peeling lamination on the keys. I was wrestling with the desire to make a real difference in the world and with the desire to hold onto my comfort.

One afternoon while I was volunteering, I saw a baby boy around six months old sitting on the floor. Although kids were usually crashing small cars or reading books in that area of the store, this boy caught my attention because he wasn't playing. He sat there with mismatched socks and a runny nose, just staring at a toy across from him with a blank expression. I looked over at his foster mother at the register. She dug through her purse on the counter and wiped her forehead, looking nearly as lethargic as the baby on the floor. I overheard her talking to the ladies up front about how she was "in over her head' and that she needed "respite care." The little boy was sick, and she was feeling too old to take care of a crying baby who refused to sleep. In a candid moment, she admitted it was too much for her, and she didn't know what to do.

As the women at the register continued to talk, I grabbed a tissue and bent down to wipe his nose. I smiled looking into his eyes and started talking to him in that high pitched coo most adults use around small children. I brought over a few trinkets in an attempt to play, but there wasn't much of a response on his end. I knew it was my time to do something. I was smitten.

"Well, maybe I can take him!" I blurted out before I had time to process what I had offered. "Let me go home and discuss this with my family," I said, more confidently than I felt, "and then I will definitely let you know tomorrow. Sound good?"

A look of surprise and then relief crossed the woman's face. She agreed.

I raced home to share the news with my family. Brian was supportive as usual, and the girls were so excited at the prospect of having a baby around. It was settled. Our family decided to jump into the deep end, to say yes to respite care, and to begin the certification process to become a foster family.

Oat Milk Matcha Latte

½ cup Oat Milk + 1 tsp matcha powder + raw sugar or a touch of honey

Add your matcha powder to a bowl or cup. Boil water and add a splash to your matcha. Whisk together. Froth your oat milk (my favorite is Oatly) and pour over your matcha mixture. Add in raw sugar or a touch of honey and whisk together. It has so many health benefits, and it will give you a natural energy boost. Enjoy!

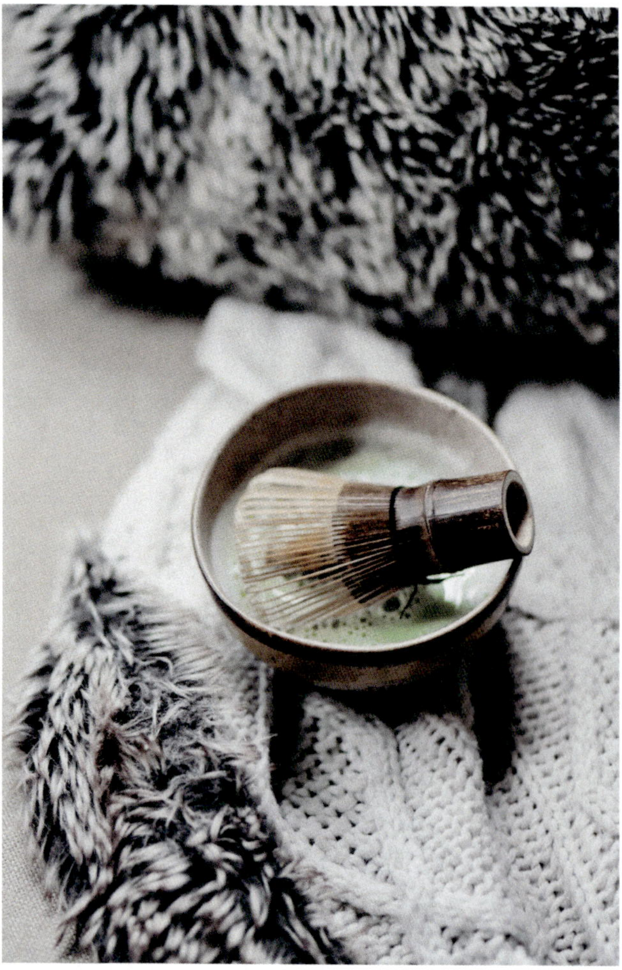

CHAPTER 5
FIRST LOVE

"If there ever comes a day when we can't be together, keep me in your heart, I'll stay there forever."
Winnie the Pooh (A.A. Milne)

The girls burst through the door after school, excited to meet the little "Gerber baby" I had described the night before. But much to their surprise, Kolton looked like anything but the beautiful, happy baby they envisioned. He was sickly pale with a constant runny nose. His hair was scraggly and growing in the shape of a rat tail down his neck. He would scream at games of peek-a-boo and acted scared most of the time. Kolton had been abandoned in a drug home when he was five months old. It would take some time for him to adjust.

It was love at first sight for Brian and me, and once the girls got past his not-so-perfect-baby looks, they fell in love with him, too. In fact, Shelby who was now in the third grade, happily shared a room with Kolton and volunteered to play games with him early in the mornings while the rest of us woke up. The girls would race home after school to squeeze him and change his clothes just because it was fun. (Back then, the girls were obsessed with their dolls, so having a live version was a novelty that never wore off.) Looking back now, I realize I couldn't have done as much as I did without their help. They treated that sweet baby boy like their own little brother.

In the few months Kolton had been in our home, his cheeks regained color, and his nose stopped running. We gave him a haircut (with permission from the county) and dressed him in tiny jeans and flannel shirts. Kolton started to respond to our games of peek-a-boo, and he began sleeping well and had a consistent feeding schedule. Much to our delight, he was full of belly laughs! We took him to the beach and to dance recitals and to my dad's house for family dinners. Suddenly, we couldn't imagine life without him.

When Kolton was nine months old, we were told by his social worker that his extended family had been found, and one of them was coming to get him. I cried every day for weeks and just kept thinking God would not let me bear this pain. I begged God to intervene and let him stay with our family. Finally, the dreaded day did come, and we had to let him go. I remember waking up and hoping it was just a bad dream. We slowly loaded the car and drove in silence until we arrived at our designated meeting place. I couldn't speak. I took a few deep breaths, fighting the lump in my throat. I prayed fast and desperate prayers - "God, give us strength. God, help me." I made Brian get Kolton out of his car seat. The car door shut, and the sudden emptiness was overwhelming. I saw his favorite, cozy blanket in the backseat, and I grabbed it and ran my hand over the silky corners where he had chewed. My heart sank, realizing I would never again get to brush the hair off his forehead as he slept. I would miss his first steps and his first day of kindergarten.

We said our quick and polite goodbyes, and I relinquished the blanket and the baby I had come to consider my own. We started the drive back home in silence, back to the empty crib and the empty highchair and the diapers we wouldn't need anymore. I took shaky breaths and kept my gaze ahead or up at the sun visor when I needed to blink away a wave of loss. All of a sudden, Brian sniffed loudly. I looked at him to see tears streaming down his face, contorted in quiet pain. I glanced in the rearview mirror to see the girls doing the same. In a collective burst, we all lost it together and cried for what felt like days. The loss of Kolton felt like a death. The pain was real and raw. It was excruciating to watch our girls grieve. Other parents actively protect their kids from pain while I was consciously bringing it into their lives. Was I screwing up my kids? In my agony, I decided, I will never do this to our family again.

Sweet and Salty Granola

Oats + Almonds + Coconut oil + Sea Salt + Honey + Coconut + Allspice + vanilla extract

Melt ½ cups coconut oil. Mix 2 cups oats, ½ cup almonds, the coconut oil, 1 tsp sea salt, 1/4 cup of honey, 1 cup coconut, 1 tsp. & ¼ allspice. Bake at 315 for 15-20 minutes until golden brown. Mix it around every 5 minutes. Let cool. You can adjust the recipe and add dried cranberries or dark chocolate. Serve in an acai bowl or as a snack. Buy some cute bags or containers for gifts to give away.

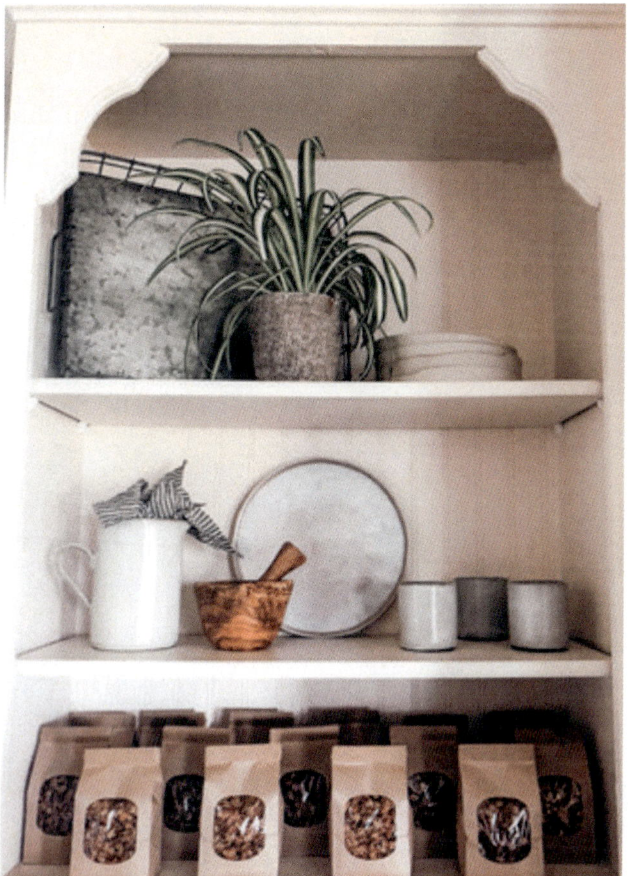

CHAPTER 6
HARD TO PLACE

"Do your little bit of good where you are; it's those little bits of good put together that overwhelm the world."

Desmond Tutu

....

Months later, we moved to Colorado, and the cloud of Kolton's absence was subsiding but still palpable. In fact, the girls even asked if we could become a foster family again. They obviously felt more resilient than I did.

One spring day while on a water break during a tennis match, I got a call from the county that there was a newborn baby boy who needed a placement. I called Brian, threw my racket in the trunk, and went straight to the hospital. Walking quickly through the sterile linoleum hallways, I inhaled that antiseptic smell, looking anxiously for the labor and delivery ward.

I heard Trever before I saw him. His cries were like no other I had ever experienced. He shrieked with a desperation that broke me in two. The nurse handed him to me, and I sat and rocked him for hours, trying in vain to feed him a few ounces of formula. He was fragile, and his tiny body was processing the drugs still in his system. I was scared. We sat in that room, two strangers sharing the same uncertainty.

Trever lived with us for nearly nine months, and in that time we had fallen madly in love with him. Since we knew child welfare's goal was for him to be placed back with his family, we had been doing consistent visits with his parents. We were rooting for them, and everything was going according to plan.

But then one day, his caseworker called me and asked if we could get together. She sat at my kitchen table, and explained something bad had happened between the parents, and she asked me if we would consider adopting him. I was shocked. The goal had always been to get him reunited back with his birth family. Adoption was nowhere on my radar.

More out of curiosity than anything else, I asked, "What would happen if I said no?"

"He'll be just fine," she said casually. "There's a long line of families waiting for the babies. I just wish there was a line of families for all of the other kids."

I was confused. "What other kids?" I questioned.

She set down her teacup.

"In Colorado, there are over 800 older kids available for adoption. I just wish someone would choose those kids."

She went on to explain that these "hard to place" kids were the ones lost in the foster care system. Sibling groups, older kids, bi-racial kids, and boys. Apparently, most people were looking to adopt babies -- and hoping for a girl on top of that. These were just the facts, the cold hard statistics. The sudden injustice of it all made me sit up straight. I thought to myself, Somebody should do something about this!

This injustice kept me up at night. I kept thinking about the fate of the sibling groups and older kids who had been forgotten. I also thought about the possibility of adopting Trever or letting a deserving, infertile couple raise him. A bittersweet conundrum. After going back and forth, I sensed God nudging me -- toward the larger injustice of tens of thousands of older children having a much lower likelihood of experiencing a forever home. I had no idea what to do next. I just knew I had to do something.

Confit Chicken with Potatoes and Demi Sauce

Quarter Chicken + Rosemary + Thyme + Cinnamon Sticks + Garlic + White Potatoes + Salt & White Pepper + Butter + Heavy Cream + Golden Yukon Potatoes

Peel potatoes and boil with salt until the water gets cloudy (don't overdo it). Poke with a fork until tender. Put the potatoes through a rice miller.

Add enough butter, enough heavy cream to make it smooth. Add salt and pepper to taste it. Be highly cautious with white pepper since it's stronger than black pepper.

Potatoes should be creamy and silky not mushy or watery.

Finish with Demi Sauce

Demi Sauce:

Carrots + Celery + Onions + Bay leaves + Thyme + Rosemary + Parsley + Black Peppercorns + beef bones + Wine

Roast 3-5 carrots, 1 bundle of celery, 3-5 large onions, and fresh garlic

Then add 1 sprig fresh thyme, rosemary, and parsley, around 3 bay leaves and black peppercorns.

Beef bones: buy from Whole Foods (ask the butcher to put to the side to pick up or find in the freezer section by the butcher section). After everybody gets roasted, throw everybody in a hot pot with water to cover all ingredients. Then add red wine and reduce.

Add water and herbs and spices. Bring to a boil and then to a simmer. Skim off the fat and "offset" (in French this means bring to nothing) and reduce down to around a qt.

Garnish: Cherry tomatoes + mushrooms + Onions + White Wine + Butter + Parsley + Salt and Pepper

A hot pan and hot oil. Saute Bella mushrooms, then onions, then tomatoes. Deglaze with dry white wine. Turn off heat and remove the pan from the heat. Add about a half a stick of cubed butter (our favorite is Kerrygold Irish Butter) and stir in small amounts at a time. Add salt and pepper to taste and throw in a little parsley. Done.

CHAPTER 7
A FACE AND A VOICE

"I believe God does his greatest work through us when we are aware of our limitations and have to trust and lean into him for outcomes that are too big for us to take on our own."

Jenni Catron

Within a few short months, incredibly, a job opened up for me to be a child-specific adoption recruiter in our county! I remember sitting in my sparse cubicle with only a cup of mismatched pens, a stack of manilla case folders, and a government-issued computer that took up the whole corner of the desk.

I read over case files one by one, flinching at each new story of abuse. I dabbed away tears and let out slow breaths so as not to be noticed in the room humming with keyboard clatter and ringing telephones. As I tried simple tasks like stirring my cup of coffee, the photos of the bruises and handprints left marks on my own mind.

Those children in the orphanage in Honduras had sunken eyes and bruises from the chemotherapy, but these marks were maliciously inflicted. I was heartbroken and simultaneously enraged. In their other snapshots, these foster kids looked like any group of kids I would pass riding bikes or playing basketball in my neighborhood. Siblings had their arms around each other -- some wore glasses, and some wore polo shirts. These kids had become invisible to the community, but now that I saw them, I couldn't look away.

I realized the power of images to engage the heart and the power of having God on my side. Brian was a pastor so he was connected to the churches. We teamed up, and I took new, dignifying, and beautiful photos of the kids. We showed them at churches, and before long, these kids were getting placed into loving families, and I thankfully worked myself out of a job.

I later learned about the Heart Gallery, a state-wide program that professionally photographed children who were waiting to be adopted. These photos and short bios toured the state (from community events to the capitol building) in a walk-through display designed to raise awareness for older youth and sibling groups needing permanent homes. The state heard about what was happening with older youth and siblings getting placed in our county, so they asked for our help.

I was excited and a little nervous to go on my first photoshoot with them. I loved getting to meet the kids.

They had cute dimples, told funny jokes, and shared their dreams for the future -- some wanted to be social workers, artists, and teachers, but all wanted the love of a family.

In between scenery changes, sometimes they would ask me, "How long will it take for you to find me a home?" I would overhear sibling groups who weren't placed together say to each other, "I hope someone will adopt all of us together." It always knocked the wind out of me. I remember thinking, if someone could just hear what I am hearing and see what I am seeing, we could get all of these kids adopted. The idea popped up in my head: If one image could grab your heart, how much more powerful would a video be?

At the very next state Heart Gallery meeting, something came up about the possibility of making videos. I can't help but think this wasn't a coincidence. Producing the segments would take coordination between the state, county recruiters, foster families, and the Heart Gallery. I was in the right place at the right time.

"Could we do the videos?" I inquired.

Within moments, Sharen Ford (who was a huge blessing to us), one of the top officials in child welfare, said yes.

The only catch was we didn't have an organization. The state was requiring we have a nonprofit - I had no clue on how to start a nonprofit or how to raise money!

We had no name, no website, no mission statement, no funding, and only a staff of one (two once Brian was named President, CEO, and future employee of the month). Obviously, God is so much bigger than I am.

Adopt Colorado Kids was founded in 2010 and followed a grassroots model. We met with local business owners, pastors, and foster families. We ran community 5Ks and recruited our own children to help us set up the Heart Gallery in venues across the state. In the early years, Brian and I worked tirelessly out of our home to be able to fund and create videos that gave kids in foster care a voice. I was convinced it was easy for people to ignore a statistic when they didn't know the kids' names or faces or when they hadn't heard their voices and their dreams. If we could just share these kids' stories, people would be compelled and would be moved to action. By the grace of God, churches stepped up, (especially Flatirons who funded the majority of the videos) and with the help of other nonprofits like Project 1:27, the number of legally-free, adoptable kids in Colorado dropped from 800 to 280.

Our organization, which started out as little more than a rash promise with good intentions, was helping children find forever families. Things started to explode. During this time, a social enterprise company from Chicago called Fox River approached us and said they wanted to team up with us to help us grow beyond Colorado. We agreed. We also teamed up with Ryan and Janet Kelly who had amazing success in Virginia with a "grasstops" approach by working through the governor's office.

Our faith continued to grow, and so did our non-profit. We went national and Adopt Colorado Kids became America's Kids Belong.

Acai Bowls

Frozen Acai + dates + coconut milk + frozen banana

Set out your frozen acai for 15 minutes to soften a bit.

Add the four ingredients in a blender. Add a bit more coconut milk if it gets too thick in the blender but you don't want it too runny either. Pour into a bowl.

Top with bananas + strawberries + blueberries + blackberries + raspberries + G's granola + toasted coconut and honey. Add in a spoonful of almond butter if you want a little protein. This is packed with antioxidants and a healthy start to your day.

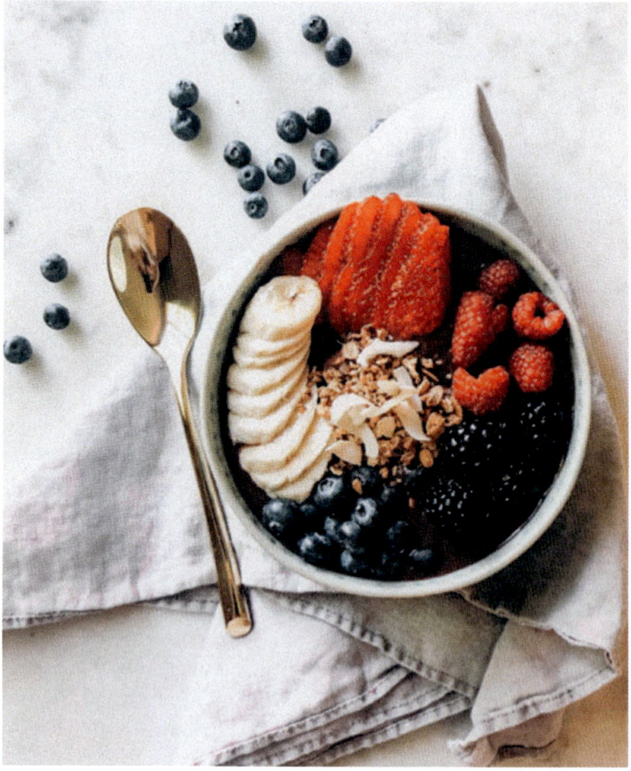

CHAPTER 8
BE MINE

"Our 'NO' will be much more difficult on them than our 'YES' will ever be on us."

Jason Johnson

....

I first met "G" (out of an abundance of caution, I will be referring to this young man only as "G") on a cold, snowy evening in February 2016. At six feet three inches tall and the only young black man in the room that evening, G stood out. His pants were a few inches too short. His green tie clashed with the buttoned-down shirt he was wearing, and his dress shoes were scuffed and noticeably well-worn. He had been invited to our annual fundraising event called Be Mine at the Westin Hotel ballroom in downtown Denver. He was in one of our programs called Dream Makers where businesses, individuals, and organizations gave practical gifts for youth aging out of foster care to help them with their career or to become independent. Some asked for cars, laptops, art supplies, or tuition money. G had asked for professional-grade, copper pots and pans.

Leaning against the wall near the DJ booth, G seemed shy. I watched him out of the corner of my eye for a few brief seconds as he stood by himself, fidgeting nervously with his phone. I walked over and introduced myself. I asked him questions and each time there would be a long pause before he eventually answered. I assumed he was just nervous. We sat at separate tables that evening so I didn't get to ask him more questions after the program started.

As the night went on, I learned from my friend Lori Bruegman that G was homeless and our organization was putting him up in a hotel. He had fallen on hard times since aging out of foster care, which is a very common scenario for most kids without a loving family or supportive community around them. G was living in a nearby motel on his last dime, feeling hopeless and considering a few last-ditch efforts at salvaging his life. He was looking to get back on his feet and was certain his culinary skills and restaurant experiences would be his ticket. But it was a hard ticket to sell considering his circumstances.

As a recipient of a Dream Makers gift, G had agreed to share his story on stage that night. I watched intently as he held tightly to the microphone in a room full of strangers. My heart ached as he shared that he never really knew what love was because of the way he was treated as a child. He had nobody and no support.

He wasn't looking for pity, he was just sharing the truth about his life.

G belonged to that group of youth who were "Hard to Place." When he went into foster care, he was a teenage male with dark-colored skin. Those were three strikes against him in the unfortunately biased game of home placement. Aging out of the foster care system was the final blow to a life that had already been unimaginably hard.

It was my turn to speak next, but I could barely move. I've heard hundreds of these stories over the years from kids in the foster-care system, and while I've always felt a deep sense of compassion for these kids, I knew I could no longer be a foster mom and do my full-time role which included a lot of travel. Something shifted that night.

I thought, what if G came to live with us? Although apprehensive at the thought of him coming to live with us, I was more afraid of what would happen to him if we didn't say yes to this opportunity. I'm sure Brian wouldn't mind! My sweet husband was no stranger to surprise, especially when it came to our foster care journey. (In fact, Brian fondly calls me "Lucy" because I have the same impulsivity of Lucille Ball in the old sitcom I Love Lucy.)

Now all I had to do was find my husband and convince him that this was a good idea. Here is a brief transcript of our conversation on the way home later that night:

"Hon, remember G?"

"Yeah."

"Well, I found out he is homeless. He is in a hotel and out of money. Would you be open to having him come live with us?"

"For how long?"

"Just a few weeks - until he gets his feet back on the ground."

"Um, sure."

"Good. Because he's coming tomorrow!"

Beets Beets Salad

Beets: Yellow beets + Red beets + Balsamic Vinegar + Vinegar

Roast beets at 400. Put in tin foil individually with salt and pepper and olive oil. Poke with a knife until tender, which usually takes about an hour. Use an old towel (or to push Julie's buttons, use her new ones) to peel off the skin, and then let cook down. Slice one inch thick. Use 3 different size cutting molds for a dripp'n (beautiful) presentation. Take your purple beets and cover with balsamic vinegar. Take your yellow beets and add in apple cider vinegar to pickle overnight.

Orange reduction: Tarragon + orange juice

Around ½ cup orange juice (Simply brand pulp-free) reduce in a small pot by ½ until syrupy or Nape (to coat the back of the spoon). Cool down and add 1 strand tarragon to the simple syrup. Put in the refrigerator overnight.

Creme fresh: Heavy cream + Buttermilk

Equal parts heavy cream and buttermilk and stir together. Put in a small bowl and add plastic on top of the cream. Push down so it's airtight. Leave for 2-3 days in the house around 70 degrees.

Shallot + Bay leaf + White wine + Salt and Pepper

Slice one shallot. Get yourself a small saucepan and add in bay leaf. Add in enough white wine and reduce by half. Cool down. Pour over the sliced shallot and season with salt and pepper.

Candied walnuts: Walnuts + White Wine + Sugar

Toast walnuts in a pan on low heat until you

smell them and then remove from heat. Get your self (G's words) a saucepan and add in equal parts sugar and water. Cook it until it becomes a simple syrup. Then add your whole walnuts. Coat walnuts then drain. Heat oven to 200. Use parchment paper on a sheet tray and spray so walnuts don't stick. Cook walnuts around 5-7 minutes until you smell them and they become dry and candy-like. Toss walnuts in a ninja to blend or crush them after they are cooled down.

Assemble: Red Beets then yellow beets, dollop on creme fresh, add orange tarragon reduction, and dust on candied walnuts. Add a couple of sprigs of fresh arugula on top and on the side of the plate for presentation. Done.

CHAPTER 9
BREAKING BREAD

"If we make space in our lives for certain kinds of people but not others, we will never know the fullness of God or understand the depths of God's love for humanity."

Heather Avis

....

G moved in with only a few tattered boxes of his possessions. He kept mostly to himself, and I learned quickly he wasn't a hugger. It was hard at first for me and Brian to set boundaries with a almost 24-year-old near stranger. For the first few weeks, I would make breakfast but G wouldn't eat. I was annoyed but when he eventually asked me if he could help make breakfast, I was happy he at least wanted to join me in the kitchen.

I really didn't know much about G at that point. One morning he told me he had put himself through Auguste Escoffier - a school of culinary arts in Boulder. He began to teach me about "Mise en Place" pronounced [me-zohn plahs], which is a French culinary term for "putting in place" or "everything in its place." This idea refers to the setup required before cooking when a chef gets out all of the kitchen tools, utensils, and ingredients and puts them together. He explained true cooking starts from there. Somehow he had already visualized a complete meal and moved swiftly from our pantry to our cupboards and then to the fridge. He narrated with each selection:

Eggs (Apparently I had bought the wrong brand)

Herbs (I needed fresh ones - not from the jar)

Garlic (He preferred fresh garlic, not minced)

Arugula

Olive oil

Applewood smoked bacon

Heirloom tomatoes

Pans (Mine were all wrong)

Knives (mine were pitiful)

He ran upstairs to go find his copper pans explaining they helped cook things evenly. G picked up a few eggs, cracked them into a hot pan with one hand and proceeded to flip them without a spatula. I saw he had the talent to be more than just "a cook." His movements were orchestrated yet smooth. He was focused, inspired, and more relaxed than I had ever seen him. The aroma of garlic, and sizzling bacon traveled throughout the house and lured Brian instinctively to the kitchen.

When we sat down at the table and began to eat, G became more vulnerable and started sharing bits of his childhood with us.

The following are accounts given with permission by G. Be advised, though. I sanitized them, but they recount real and tragic life events.

I didn't speak until I was five years old. My mom had me tested, and I was diagnosed with autism. She tried to fix me by "detoxing" my food, which would have been hard since most of our meals were packages of ramen, fast food, or sometimes southern cooking when they had more money. She seemed to care for me since she was concerned with my health, but there was never any affection for me, no encouragement, and they stopped celebrating my birthday when I was 10.

My mom was living by the moment and had no routines. We were hungry a lot and many times she didn't pay the bills so the electricity or water was shut off. By the time I was in the 4th grade, we had moved hella crazy on the daily - different apartments in the ghetto, a rented house in the hood, an extended-stay hotel or the local motel, or homeless shelters when things were really bad. The worst scenario was the van. I figured out we moved so much--from state to state--because my mom's boyfriend was running from the law. I also figured out my mom sold herself, and that's why there were so many strange men she was with no matter where we were. I now know I saw way too much as a kid.

Admittedly, it was hard to eat. Even though the eggs were perfectly runny and the crispy bacon balanced so well with the peppery arugula, my fork had ceased to make trips to my mouth. Hearing these stories, I understood life was anything but routine for G. Food was scarce. Affection was even more scarce. And he spent most of his childhood starving for both. Instinctively and without so much as a look, Brian and I knew to let him keep talking. We didn't know if or when he would ever open up like this again.

They beat me a lot. They'd tie me up naked and beat me with a belt, a fist, or anything within reach. I had very few friends and no girlfriends so my mom made me watch porn to "fix" me. They would lock me in my room, sometimes for days, without food. There were times the abuse was too much. I remember picking up a big knife as a six or seven-year-old kid and holding it to my heart to kill myself. My sister saw me holding the knife to my chest and burst out crying,

"G, what are you doing? Please don't do that. I need you!"

I listened to my sister and put down the knife.

School was hard because of all the crazy stuff

happening to me, and I was always in trouble because I couldn't communicate well. I would get so frustrated being misunderstood so I would explode, throwing chairs, getting in fights and being expelled, even as a kindergartner. At the end of fourth grade, my mom took me out of school and said she would homeschool me. I knew my mom was lying and wouldn't even try to homeschool me. I would still try to teach myself to read by looking at comic books, but I could only read short words.

Instead of going to school my mom made me sell candy with my sister outside grocery stores to "raise money for autism." The days were so flipp'n hot in the summer and freez'n in the winter. We hated working and wanted to play like all the other kids. We did raise a lot of money because people always said how cute we were. But the money didn't go to autism; my mom and her boyfriend used all of the money for booze, weed, rent, and food.

He shook his head from the memory of those wasted days, took one last oversized bite of breakfast, and stood to clear his plate in the sink. My head and heart were reeling.

My job as a foster mom is never to "fix" anyone; rather it's to give them a seat at our table and let them know they are enough. I don't know what it's like to go hungry or to be abused, but I do know something about brokenness, and I'm so thankful Jesus says to me, "Julie you are enough. Come as you are, and you will always have a seat at my table."

Sunnyside-Up Toast

Yummy bread + Avocado mayo + Crofters superfruit spread + Applewood smoked bacon + Arugula + Avocado + Organic heirloom tomatoes + Sunnyside organic egg on top

Toast your bread

Combine equal parts avocado mayo and Crofters superfruit spread

Cook bacon at 450 until crispy (he doesn't use a timer and just smells things to know when it's ready)

Hot pan, add olive oil and salt and pepper

Crack the egg and let it go until it is no longer runny in the middle. Don't flip it. Throw it in the oven for a minute or two if you're nervous it's not cooked in the middle. Layer it up and enjoy!

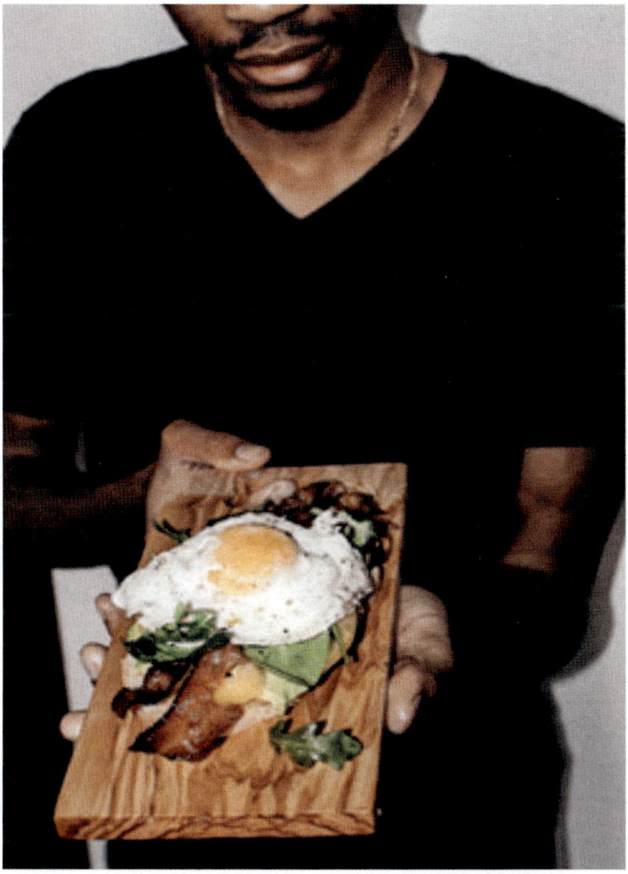

CHAPTER 10
SCRAPS OF LIFE

"Food is not only meant to nourish the body but also the soul. It is the element in every culture and is a universal language which brings people together to fellowship and commune."

The Little Bird Bakeshop, Fort Collins, CO.

(One of my favorite coffee shops)

We didn't have a lot in common. Except for a few musicians we both liked listening to, our time together revolved around going grocery shopping and cooking. Making a connection with foster kids can sometimes be challenging, but food would always bring us together. Most foster kids have food insecurities and need constant reminders there will always be enough. I never liked our girls to have food in their bedrooms, but with foster kids the rules changed, and I encouraged it so they wouldn't ever have the fear of being hungry in our home. I made it a priority to take all our kids to the grocery store, let them pick out foods they liked, and we would always eat dinner together. Food builds trust and opens a way for healing to take place just by making them feel safer. With G's love for cooking I would convince him to go with me to Sprouts, one of our favorite grocery stores, and then we would cook together.

He would pull together a menu in his head and throw in the cart an array of things like exotic pears, usual spices, fresh herbs, black garlic, and vanilla beans (never the imitation vanilla from the bottle). I wasn't much of a cook. Creating a charcuterie board was about the extent of my culinary skills. When G and I came home from the store, I would get my apron on with high hopes of learning some of his techniques, but nine times out of ten he was quickly annoyed with me for either asking too many questions, or for the smell of my perfume, or for not chopping something fast enough. I would then sit at our kitchen island, with my glass of wine -- out of the way -- watching him in his happy place. Sometimes in between chopping and sauteing, he would let a little scrap of his life fall on the counter between us.

> When I was a teenager I remember staying up late at night so I could watch cooking shows. I used to hide a towel under the door to block the light from the TV and would turn up the volume to drown out the fighting inside my home and the gunshots outside in the streets. I watched hours of Rachael Ray, Julia Child, Lidia Bastianich, and Alton Brown on the

Food Network while fantasizing about eating fine cuisine someday. It was my escape.

Watching G in the kitchen was a magical combination of mastery, unrestrained attention to detail, and beautiful artistry. Not only did his food taste delicious, but the presentation was consistently like something out of a magazine. In those rare moments afterward, at the kitchen table, we would share meals and stories. Each gave me one more glimpse of the hazy picture of his life before us.

We continued to be on the move from Colorado to California, Indiana, Illinois, the south side of Chicago (which seemed like it's own state worth mentioning outside of Illinois), then on to Nevada, our family eventually landed back in Denver. I was 16 and my sister was 14. Within a few months of returning to Denver, my sister got placed in foster care. I felt heartbroken and confused. Nobody explained what was happening. Then a few days later I was back at selling candy at the local Walmart in Littleton. My mom picked me up, asked for the money I raised, and then drove me over to the county courthouse. She didn't say anything in the car, and I knew something was off. My mom took me inside and had all of my clothes in a trash bag and left me. At the time I didn't know why she left me, but now I know that since my sister was placed in foster care days earlier, my mom didn't want the police involved. She decided to give me up instead of having me taken away. I still remember what I was wearing that day my mom dropped me off: a black and red jacket from the Goodwill store, the only t-shirt I owned, my jeans had rips in them not because they were in style like nowadays but because they were so old and my shoes were so beat-up that the souls literally flapped when I walked. My hair was nappy and hadn't had a good wash or haircut in months, maybe even years. My mind went blank at that moment. I was sixteen years old, and that was the last time I ever saw my mom.

Within a short time of moving into our home, I found myself bonding with G. He was working through so much emotionally and relationally those days, and I desperately wanted him to find healing. He needed to get his finances in order and address the trauma from his past with some new coping skills and behavior management. He was a handful, but I quickly shifted from wanting to give him a place to stay, to thinking about how much I would love to be his mom. I put his picture up in the dining room with the rest of our family photos and fantasized about the day he would be adopted. I saw the happy ending.

Ribollita - Tuscan Vegetable Soup and Homemade Croutons

Carrots + Celery + Onion + Fresh Garlic + Swiss Chard + Zucchini + Tomatoes + Mushrooms + Garlic + Fresh thyme and Rosemary sprigs + Olive oil + Great Northern Beans or Navy beans + Salt & Pepper + Red Chili flakes + Parmesan Cheese + Ciabatta or Italian bread

Wash all the vegetables and chop them up however you like them. In a large dutch oven get your pan hot and add your olive oil. Add in your fresh garlic until it is fragrant and light brown. Throw in your carrots, celery, and onions (we used a yellow onion). Keep stirring it for around 5 minutes. Add in your swiss chard, zucchini, tomatoes (my favorite brand is Cento - San Marzano) and your thyme and rosemary sprigs plus your can of great northern beans with the liquid. Add in salt, pepper, and red pepper flakes. Add around 3-4 cups of stock or water and cook another 25 minutes until the vegetables are tender. Turn off the heat and take out the fresh herbs.

Croutons:Tear apart your Ciabatta bread or

just add the slices to a cookie sheet. Drizzle olive oil over the bread. Season with salt and pepper. Place in the oven at 375 and stir or turn the bread over half way through until golden brown to give it that crunch. Pour the soup and garnish with robust olive oil, shaved parmesan cheese, and toasted croutons or slice of bread. So yummy!

CHAPTER 11
OUR OWN HELL'S KITCHEN

"You were made for the place where your real passion meets compassion, because there lies your real purpose."

Ann Voskamp

At this point in our lives, our oldest daughter, Elle, and her new husband, Caleb, were living in our basement while they looked for a place of their own. And our youngest daughter, Shelby, had just returned from college. It was a rare moment when we were all living under the same roof—Brian and I with our grown, young adult daughters, our dog Avery, our new son-in-law, their two cats and now G. Avery and the cats were running amuck, the kitchen was always a mess, G was stressed out with the unpredictable schedules of people coming and going at all hours. I was going through menopause, having hot flashes and frantically trying every supplement known to mankind to help my thinning hair. Brian is such a peacemaker and prefers to avoid conflict so he would often hide in his office, hoping the madness would soon end. It was chaos. Total chaos.

At about six months in, the "honeymoon phase" was officially over. Weeks went by and things felt very off and distant with G. He worked but would come home and spent most of his time in his dark room. We offered to have him join us for dinner, but he would just grab a snack and head to his room to eat. I was seeing that G didn't like it when I would pat him on the back or surprise him with something or change the routine in the home. We wanted him to experience family outings so we tried taking him to the zoo, movies, and even a trip to Nashville. He hated all of them and would literally run away or just go sit in the car waiting for us to take him home. I would bring tea to his room, and he wouldn't thank me but instead would say something like "you sure pack on that makeup." Whenever I had my Christian music on, he would quickly put his headphones on to drown out my music. We were both figuring out that not only was our skin color different, but so were our religious beliefs, hobbies, and book choices. The way we saw the world couldn't be more opposite.

In spite of all this, we would stay up late watching cooking shows, Bernie Mac, or his favorite rappers on YouTube. I actually enjoyed his company except for the random comments he would make that would hurt my feelings like, "Have you ever tried charcoal toothpaste? It would help your yellow teeth look whiter." Or touching the back of my arm, he would then say "It feels like jello." I was always offended but chalked it up to nobody taking the time to teach him about social skills.

With all our previous foster kids, Elle was the nurturing and incredibly patient one but wasn't able to get close to G because of his emotional distance. Shelby—hands down the most fun-loving member of our family who can connect with anyone—admitted she would get frustrated and take it personally when her cheery "Good Morning, G!" was met with silence and not so much as a glance. He was distant, cold, sad, and mostly angry.

We had been foster parents for years, but it was mostly for drug-exposed babies or younger kids. And though we had fostered a 17-year-old boy who was a handful, he was mostly pleasant. We were more used to screaming babies coming off of drug addiction than we were screaming, angry young men. Both were hard to hear, but we knew what to do for the babies and kids. Not only had we no training on trauma or experience dealing with someone who had been taught to run from their problems, we also had no training in recognizing his behaviors as anything other than trauma. There were triggers, fear and pain every which way he turned.

If G had something that would trigger a painful experience or he didn't feel safe, he would start screaming the f-word at the top of his lungs, slam doors, throw something breakable that would shatter against the wall. Sometimes he would jump out of my moving care or he'd punch a hole in the wall and go into a full rage. I was so scared when he was raging, but out of instinct I would just grab him tightly and try to hug him until he calmed back down. Sometimes it would take hours to get him regulated, and then he was able to share what triggered him. My heart melted every time I looked into his big brown eyes and listened to him process his pain and share some of his traumatic experiences that defined his childhood. I was the one hearing the story behind the behaviors, and it gave me more grace and compassion towards him. When I heard horrible things that were said to him and listened to the details of his brutal beatings, I had no advice or wisdom. I just sat there holding his hand and tears would stream down our faces. I never had the right words, but I cared and tried to suffer alongside him.

Fresh Herb Roasted Tomatoes

Grape tomatoes + fresh rosemary + fresh thyme + garlic + kosher salt + black pepper + oil

Preheat the oven to 400 degrees. Over the stove top, add your oil to a hot pan and then throw in the rest of the ingredients above. Cook for 2-3 minutes and then put into the oven for 4 minutes. Serve over chicken, pasta, avocado toast or on toasted bread and cheese for an appetizer.

CHAPTER 12
G: ON MY OWN

"Loneliness and the feeling of being unwanted is the most terrible poverty." Mother Teresa

I was afraid to be in foster care, and I was scared to be back in school. I hadn't been in school since the 4th grade. I could barely read, and I didn't know what group to be in since there were cliques and gangs everywhere. Most of my peers were learning how to drive, but I wasn't allowed to get my license since I was a foster kid.

I kept it together during the day at school but cried myself to sleep at night. I was moved to 3 different foster homes and one group home so that meant three different high schools. I was constantly getting bullied, and I was failing every class except for one: Home Economics. One of my teachers, who was called "Coach" by the rest of the students, saw my grades and started asking how I could be failing all of his classes except for the "A" I had in Home Economics. Coach took the time to listen to me. He saw I had a natural talent in the kitchen, and he helped me receive the extra learning support I needed so I could graduate high school - even though it took me an extra year to do it.

I got a rep at school for my baked goods that I made in class. So to put some money in my pocket, I didn't eat my portion of the desserts we made in my class, and I started slinging them after school. I also figured out at the group home that nobody wanted to do their chores so I hustled, got them done, and got even more money to buy clothes, shoes, and a PlayStation. All the things I didn't get as a kid.

Eventually, at twenty-one years of age, I aged out of foster care and was feeling unprepared and alone in this world until I met you guys.

Manchego Infused Oil Tapas

Olive oil + Fresh Garlic + Oregano + Thyme + Red Chili Flakes + Black Peppercorn

Pour one cup olive oil into a hot pan and 3 crushed garlic cloves. Add in fresh oregano and thyme or around 1 tsp of dried oregano and thyme.

Add a pinch of red chili flakes (around ½ tsp) and some crushed black peppercorn.

Cook for 2-4 minutes. Then let it cool completely. Shave your manchego cheese and cut off the rind. Pour the cheese over the room- temperature oil mixture. Stir in and let marinade in the refrigerator 4-8 hrs. Serve over your favorite toasted bread or crackers. Delicious appetizer!

CHAPTER 13
"TRAUMATISM"

"I believe that we humans are all the same -- we want to feel loved, that our life has purpose and meaning, that we are seen and heard, that we have gifts to offer the world, that we are worthy and enough, that our words and actions are meaningful, that we Belong, and that we are good. In other words, we want to know that we matter."

Matthew Emerzian

....

G had been living with us for almost one year when we got our popcorn one evening and sat down to watch the movie, Temple Grandin. It's a fabulous true-life story about a young woman with autism who learns to navigate life, including several layers of higher education. The movie highlighted how Temple could easily master intellectual and mechanical challenges but struggled with social situations. During the movie, Brian and I kept exchanging glances and squeezing each other's hands every time something reminded us of G. We had always wondered if there was something beyond his trauma, but we had never been able to pinpoint why there were so many meltdowns.

Brian went to bed before the credits started to roll that night, but G lingered on the sofa. I asked him, "Does anything in that movie resonate with you? Were there particular scenes you could relate to?"

"Yes, all of it," he quickly replied. "I told you I have autism."

I was reeling. How could I have missed this? I remembered his stories from childhood, but I guess I had thought everything I had witnessed was trauma not autism. The look on my face must have conveyed my confusion.

"I said that when I first came to live here," he said matter of factly before standing up and heading to bed.

I sat alone on the couch completely stunned. I felt horrible! I was embarrassed that, as someone trying to step into the "mom" role in his life, I hadn't at least figured this out on my own, particularly after he had outright told me. Suddenly everything made sense.

Now I understood:

why he took everything we said so literally;

why he had a hard time regrouping after something was out-of-sync or off-schedule;

why he didn't speak until he was five years old and has trouble communicating his feelings, especially when he's angry;

why his room was his sacred space, and how disruptive it was for me to enter his space to drop off his shoes or mail or to slightly move anything out of its spot;

why he had no problem talking at full-volume in public or making honest and hurtful comments;

why he was sensitive to light, smells and touch;

why he doesn't like giving or receiving any kind of affection from us;

why he missed so many social cues.

I felt like I had failed. I wish I had seen it sooner. Most days, we just didn't have the tools to know what to do so we all just walked around on eggshells. Obviously, dealing with the ramifications of G's trauma added a layer of complexity to his presence in our home. But I missed—or dismissed—the fact that we were dealing with more than trauma. We thought for sure G's autism diagnosis was a lie told to him early in his childhood. It seemed like an easy excuse for him to hold a sign and beg for money outside of the local grocery store as a kid. Who would say no to a cute, poor kid with autism asking for money? He told us every single cent he raised went towards something other than his medical treatment. So we assumed it was all made up, and we chalked up G's quirks and fits of rage as symptoms of trauma. We were wrong -- at least partly wrong.

Once we fully acknowledged G's autism diagnosis, we made a few adjustments in our home. We extended extra grace upon grace and made a few helpful accommodations like buying a weighted blanket to wrap around him when he got worked up and to help with his sleep. I started making lists so he could remember important things. I communicated more when routines or systems were changing in the home. We also helped G establish a consistent routine with his work schedule, and we paid him to do chores in our home to help him cover his expenses. And for the first time, we created household rules and established a monthly schedule on his calendar for all of his bills. Boundaries were established, and everything was written down in a clear and simple way.

Over time, I have lowered some of my expectations and increased my compassion. It still isn't easy. I fail most days with patience. I forget to write things down which frustrates him. I am still spontaneous and throw out last minute plans and forget that he prefers his days to look like Groundhog Day. I struggle with the way he views the world and the way the world views him, but I'm learning to honor G for who God has created him to be with all of the beauty, complexity, and creativity he brings to our home and to the world around us. He belongs.

Sweet & Spicy Barba"cola" Tacos Topped with Marinated Vegetables

Chuck Roast + Kombucha + Chipotle adobo paste + Oranges + White Onion + Garlic + Oregano + Cumin + Brown Sugar + Beef Broth + Salt and whole pepper grounds

Chop one white onion, one bulb garlic, some oregano, two large handfuls of brown sugar, around 3 tablespoons cumin, salt, and pepper. Mix this up.

Take one pound chuck roast and cut into large cubes and place in a large bowl with the above ingredients.

In a blender, blend your chipotle adobo paste and a bottle of Kombucha (Cola flavor revive) and around half of a cup of beef broth. Add to the dry ingredients above. Squeeze 3-4 oranges into the bowl and throw in leftover oranges for flavor. Add salt and pepper. Cover with plastic or a lid and marinate all of the above overnight.

Get your pan and your oil hot. Sear the chuck

roast on all sides. Then add your marinade and bring it to a boil. Throw it in the oven for 285 for around 4 hours. Tear apart the meat.

Homemade tortillas: Fresh ground masa + warm water + salt

Follow amounts on the bag of masa to create dough for tortillas. Spray tortilla maker and add parchment paper so it doesn't stick to the pan.

Topping: Cilantro + White onions + Fresh lime + Avocado

Optional Pickled Vegetable Topping: Carrots + Jalapeno Peppers + Onions + Vinegar + Bay leaves + Garlic + Pepper

Chop the below vegetables and set aside in a small bowl:

1-2 carrots

2 jalapeño peppers

1 small white onion

In a small saucepan throw everybody in the pot (G's words) around 2 cups vinegar, 1-2 bay leaves, 2 cloves garlic, and some black peppercorns. Bring to a boil then pour over your chopped vegetables to marinade overnight.

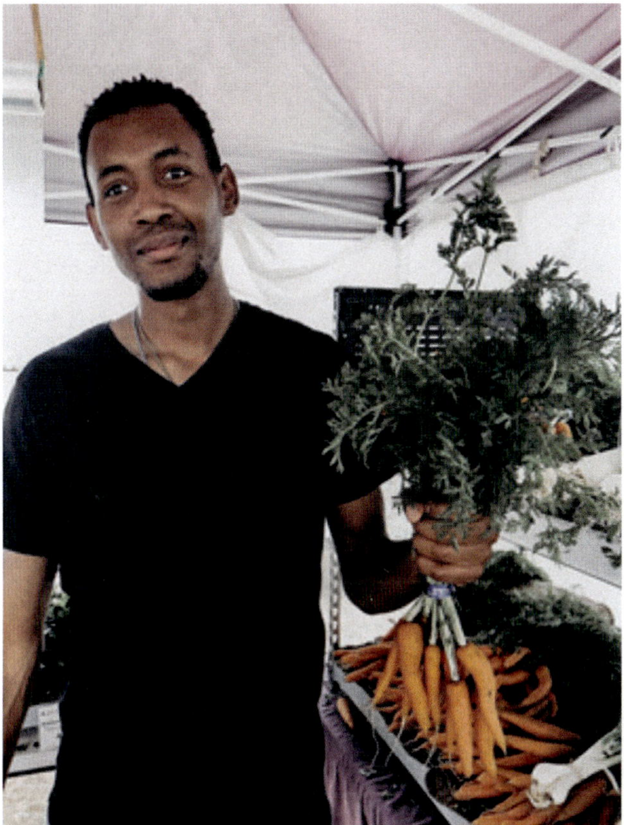

CHAPTER 14
SELFLESS LOVE

> "To love at all is to be vulnerable. Love anything and your heart will certainly be wrung, and possibly be broken… the only place outside heaven where you can be perfectly safe from all the dangers and perturbations of love is hell."
>
> —C.S. Lewis

That few weeks G was going to stay with us has turned into over three years now. Even though things remain up and down with G, we still love him deeply and have tried talking to him about adoption. He has made it very clear he doesn't want to be adopted, even though we have treated him like our very own son. It's an ache in my heart to be continually rejected by him. He never calls me mom. He doesn't even acknowledge me on Mother's Day. Because of his autism, he rarely eats dinner with us, and instead, heads up to his room to spend time alone. He comes to us only when he needs something from us. He runs away (temporarily) when he's mad or filled with shame over the poor choices he's made. He completely disregards my instructions or the cautions I bring to his attention out of protection for his well-being.

Even so, God continues to give me love towards G. It has been the most humbling experience to help run a non-profit that works (in part) to get kids adopted and to have the one kid who doesn't want to be adopted. Even though he's a young man, I just thought he would want to have a mom and family no matter what age he is. I have had to swallow my pride and give up my hope that all my efforts would end in a beautiful adoption story.

But our story isn't at the end. We're in the middle of it somewhere, and I have learned that my goal shouldn't have been about an official adoption. It's about giving G a place where he feels like he belongs: a place where he is safe and can grow and heal at his pace. And that is what is happening. G is slowly healing. His meltdowns are less frequent. He brings me tea when I'm sick. His mood is consistently lighter, and he has hope. He has become tender and has a gentleness about him. G actually enjoys being with me in the kitchen now, and we are working together to sell his spices, sling'n spices as he puts it.

I used to ask him to take care of my plants and flowers when I traveled and would come home to them all being dead. Now, he not only takes care of my plants, but he also cares for the one I bought him for his room! Previously, when I'd return home from a trip, he used to not speak to me, and it felt like he was punishing me for leaving. Maybe he didn't think I would come back. It would take hours or even days for him to warm up to me. Now I can go to his room after a week of being gone, and I can ask for a hug and get one. I can ask questions, and he's willing to share with me what his week looked like. I still have to remind him to ask me about my life, but it's getting better. He's made strides in learning to self regulate, which is huge.

Living with G has been a helpful window into the heart of God, as well as a mirror into my own soul and the soul of humanity. I notice when God offers refuge, we often run away. When God offers comfort, we push hard or fight back. When God offers love and forgiveness, we often hide in pain and shame. When God offers affection through the arms of others, we have a tendency to keep those people at arms-length.

My pursuit of G has taught me more about the love of God than I ever would have learned otherwise. God has slowly been teaching me about pure love. The kind of love you're willing to give away no matter what you receive in return. I have learned to keep my motives in-check as I show my love to G. Most days, I'm able to give love freely knowing there might not be a loving exchange in return, but there are still days when I'm left hoping for something in return.

Growth and healing for G look different than I could've imagined, and it has looked different for me, too. I've also come to learn that progress can't be measured the same way for everyone. As each day passes, his way of developing and taking steps of wholeness can be so easy to miss, but I see them.

Simple and Raw Protein Balls

Dates + Almonds + Cashews + Dark Chocolate + Sea Salt

Toast a handful of almonds and a handful of cashews (or walnuts) over high heat and keep moving it around. Once there's a nutty smell, take it off immediately. Let the nuts completely cool so they don't melt the chocolate when you add that in. Chop up the nuts in the food processor for 30-

40 seconds with 1 tsp. sea salt and ¾ of a cup of chocolate chips (my favorite are Chocolove from Boulder, Colorado) Take out and set aside in a bowl. Add around 40 dates in a food processor and mix until it all starts sticking together and clumps into a ball. Take the dates out and roll up into balls. Cover with the chocolate, sea salt, and nut mixture. Makes a great quick healthy snack

or even gifts to give away. Makes around 18 balls.

CHAPTER 15
BE BRAVE

"Ask Jesus what He wants from you and be brave."

Pope Francis

....

I stepped out and took a risk. Sometimes recklessly, sometimes thoughtfully, almost always with fear. This is what bravery required of me - moving beyond my life of comfort and security and into a life of purpose, obedience, and passion by caring for the vulnerable. I have learned to not run from pain but rather to lean in where I see pain and brokenness... If you follow God's call for your life, there's really no running from pain. Rather, it's walking straight into it knowing God is there.

No part of my life has gone exactly according to plan. My stories are bittersweet – from the children I met in orphanages, to our foster babies and kids, and even with G. I still feel inadequate to be G's foster mom. I'm learning how to navigate his special needs, and to top it off, being a white mom to a black young man sometimes feels overwhelming. I see his fears and now they have become mine. I am left at the feet of Jesus feeling broken, seeking wholeness, and needing his strength. But I will take that day after day instead of a life of comfort. I could have missed all of this, and I am thankful God used all of these kids' lives and their stories to change me and grow my heart as I loved them. Pursuing hearts has taught me so much about God's love and his constant pursuit of all of us.

I wanted to tell my story with its imperfections and heartbreak because I believe in the power of redemption. I am not qualified. I am not special. You don't have to be either.

There is a call on your life, and it's not to be comfortable. I encourage you to get still. Be silent and sit in God's presence. I guarantee, when you let God transform your heart and when you lay your life down, you will come alive and live the life you were meant to live.

So, what is your purpose?

What are your passions?

What injustice makes you angry?

What keeps you up at night?

What makes your eyes light up and your heart come alive?

Whether it's foster care, human trafficking, racism, or any other worthy cause, decide to fight for justice and live a life that champions the vulnerable.

My friends, to love will always be risky. But giving a child a chance to experience safety, belonging and love, that's a risk I'm willing to take and I hope you will too.

***

Finally, my story would be incomplete without the blind devotion of my loving husband, the selflessness of my daughters, and the dedication of the army of adoption/foster-care warriors across the country. Together we fight every day to make sure every kid has a place to belong.

Join us.

*****

Through America's Kids Belong, you can:

- Advocate for kids waiting for a family by sharing one of our I Belong Project videos on social media or donate to help us create more videos. These are beautiful love stories of children in the US just waiting to be chosen. Check them out here: https://www.americaskidsbelong.org. There are around 440,000 children in the foster care system and around 125,000 who are legally free and waiting to be adopted.

- Become a Dream Maker and support a youth who has aged out of foster care: https://www.dreammakersproject.org.

Every year approximately 25,000 youth "age out" of the foster care system when they turn 18, without a family and without the skills to make it on their own.

- Support one of our aging-out youth (including G's spices) by buying their products or services.
https://store.dreammakersproject.org
- Become a foster or adoptive parent.
- Wrap around a family who has taken in a child. Make a meal, go do their laundry, or offer to do respite care.
- Help solve this crisis as a business leader, creative leader, faith leader, or government leader.

Seoul Sliders

Pork Shoulder + Sauce + Pickled cucumbers + Brioche Bun + Soy Sauce + Garlic

Sauce: Mayo + Gochujang (Korean Chili Sauce)

Around one cup of mayo and about one tbsp chili sauce. It should look more orange than red. Taste it to see if you want more chili sauce for it to be more slamm'n.

Pickled Cucumbers: Vinegar + Cinnamon stick + Sugar

Bring to a boil around 16 ounces of vinegar, one cinnamon stick, and around one cup cane sugar. Pour over thinly sliced cucumbers. Cover with tin foil, and then leave a little open to air it out. Mason jars work great. Pickle for a day or two in the fridge.

Sofito: Fuji Apple + White onion + Ginger + Garlic

Add a small amount of oil to your hot pan. Add one chopped fuji apple first, then sweat it out. Take out apples and repeat with one chopped onion, a little bit of ginger and some garlic. Add enough oil to cover 1/3 of the pan and throw it in the oven at 285 for one hour.

Cut pork into chunks, equal sizes then add to a hot pan with hot oil and sear all sides of the pork. Then add marinade and water to cover half of the pork. Bring to a boil and cover with heavy-duty plastic and then tin foil on top to keep moisture in. Hit it at 285 until tender for around 6 hrs. The juice will reduce slightly. Carefully tear apart with tongs.

Toast slider bun bread - broil until golden brown

Buns, condiments, pork then pickled cucumbers on top. Done.

G's "Must-Have" Ingredients for Your Kitchen.

Hopefully, this list of basics to keep around the kitchen will help you as it has helped me.

- Fresh Garlic
- Onions
- Celery
- Carrots
- Campari Tomatoes (or Canned Tomatoes)
- Fresh Bella Mushrooms
- Organic Eggs (or Brown Eggs)
- Chicken Stock / Broth
- Beef Stock
- Veggie Stock
- Red & White Wine
- Distilled Apple Cider Vinegar
- Sherry Vinegar
- Soy Sauce

- Olive Oil
- Avocado Oil
- Canola Oil
- Kosher Salt
- Pepper (whole peppercorns to crack & grind)
- Fresh Herbs: Thyme, Rosemary, Oregano, Sage, Cilantro
- Dry Spices: Turmeric, Cayenne Pepper, Nutmeg, Cinnamon, Thyme, Rosemary, Bay Leaves, Oregano
- Mayo (organic or avocado mayo)
- Hot Sriracha Chili Sauce

ABOUT THE AUTHOR:

Julie Mavis is a cofounder of America's Kids Belong and creator of two national programs, Dream Makers and the I Belong Project. She lives in Windsor, Colorado, and works alongside her husband Brian and their black lab, Avery. Her daughters (and now friends) Elle and Shelby, live nearby with their loved ones and are pursuing their dreams—some of which happen to revolve around foster care and adoption, too. In addition to the work she loves, Julie enjoys walks with Brian and Avery, time in the kitchen with G, happy hour, snuggling with Elle's foster babies, and experiencing God in the silent and simple things in life.

Made in the USA
Monee, IL
24 January 2021